To The Davis Family, Wishing you all of God's many ble

War and Violence, Eternal Life or Death

Lennise G. Morris

Germaine Publications

War and Violence, Eternal Life or Death
Published by Germaine Publications
2480 Briarcliff Road, #339
Atlanta, GA 30329
(770) 498-0047
E-mail: lennisem@bellsouth.net

Cover Design by Toni Scott-Daniel

Unless otherwise indicated, all Scripture quotations are from the King James Version of the Bible.

For emphasis, the author has placed quotations from the Bible in italics.

Second printing 2002

Library of Congress Card Number: 97-94292

ISBN 0-9651334-1-9

Printed in the United States of America

This book is dedicated
to all those
who love the Lord.

Contents

Acknowledgements

Much appreciation is given to Dan Hayes, the founder and executive director of Atlanta Community Ministries. Thanks for believing in my vision and making this second printing possible.

I am thankful for the family members who encouraged and supported my ministry:

my wonderful parents, Aris and Zelma Cager Morris,
my grandmother, Rose Cager,
Donald and Barbara Dyson Cager Sr.,
Roland and Maxine Hill Cager,
Larry and Dorothy Glynn Cager,
Eric Cager, Donna Cager, and Elois Cager Brooks.

Sincere appreciation is given to Emile J. Labat III and the Boissiere-Labat Family Funeral Services in New Orleans, Louisiana.

Although there are many people who helped me along the way, it is impossible for me to list each name. Much gratitude is given to those special friends who provided significant contributions:

Timothy and Janice Ogle Bennett, Leslie Caldwell, Bernice and Kevin Dickey, Angela and Guy Heath, Charmaine and Kenneth Johnson, Andrea and Randall McHenry, Rene and Tresonne J. Peters, Toni Scott-Daniel, Gale Solomon, Tanya Turner, Susan Winchester, and David Wyatt.

Preface

This book, *War and Violence, Eternal Life or Death*, was written under the anointing of the Holy Spirit, geared to helping those who are in battle and in spiritual warfare. Today, we face many challenges in our jobs, homes, communities, social groups, political organizations, and neighboring countries. We war against one another, but we must know that the main culprit is Satan. Ephesians 6:12 states, *"For we wrestle not against flesh and blood, but against principalities, against powers, against the rulers of darkness of this world, against spiritual wickedness in high places."*

It is not a fight of black against white; it is not a war of nation against nation, nor of religion against religion. Rather, it is a war against the enemy Satan. We have allowed Satan to cause dissension: among the races fueling racism; among the sexes, causing men and women to war against each other; among the religious denominations fostering hostilities and stereotypes; and within the family, resulting in cruelty and violence. We are also at war with drugs in our inner cities and urban communities, where we face drug warlords, drug dealers, and drug users. Tempted and succumbing to drugs, many men and women destroy their bodies and poison their minds.

All of these hateful and wicked devices come from the pits of hell to separate, destroy, and devour our souls. It's time that we take control and realize who the true enemy is. Satan's ultimate goal is to destroy and rob our souls subjecting us to the pits of eternal damnation. God's ultimate purpose for us is to be saved and walk a righteous life so that we may have eternal life. So, the next time we have a struggle on the job with our bosses, our spouses, with higher ranking authority, we should recognize who the culprit is, remembering that God comes to give us peace. God's word says to love one another and not to hate. God's word also instructs us to rejoice when persecuted and pray for those who use us.

I hope the following prose pieces, short stories, and poems illustrate the many ways God's people come under attack, and show plainly that the solution is to surrender to God. For God will direct our paths. Even though we may suffer afflictions or trials in life, we should count it all joy. Romans 5:3-4 states that "*. . . we glory in tribulations also; knowing that tribulation worketh patience; And patience, experience; and experience, hope. . . .*"

It is we who wait on the Lord who shall prosper. Remember, Jesus came to save those who are lost. I hope the following writing will help you understand that in this world, we are at war, not against flesh and blood but against principalities, powers, rulers of darkness, and spiritual wickedness.

"As it is written, For thy sake we are killed all the day long; we are accounted as sheep for the slaughter."

Romans 8:36

Chapter 1

✦✦✦✦

War, the Vibrant Soldier Survives

Prologue

*M*any times we are falsely persecuted for a wrong which has been committed. In society where the justice system has proven to employ injustice, many men and women have been convicted for crimes undone. In our lives, some of us have been ostracized or persecuted, merely because of race, our belief system in God, socioeconomic levels, and cultural values. As Christians, we are tested constantly to prove our faith in God. I can attest to this fact by the great challenges of faith in my life, from being falsely persecuted in social arenas to work environments. It's not just a matter of the color of your skin or economic level, but more of a moral standard judged by mankind. We are at war with our neighbors by devices used by Satan which are employed into our minds like one race of people is better than another or a poor person is second class to a rich person. We have vacated biblical principles of judging mankind. If we would base our moral values and standards on biblical principles, we would have a better world system. Too many times, God's people fail at faith when others judge them. Acts 5:29 NRSV states, ". . . *We must obey God rather* *than any human authority."*

Many times God allows the trials in our lives to make us stronger and to seek God's will more. So, the next time you find yourself in a challenging situation, seek God first for the solution. God is looking for warriors, not wimps. God is calling a new nation of stronger men and women to walk boldly in God's glory. We, as Christians, have a job to do. We must witness, testify, and help save souls by leading them to the kingdom. Although you may suffer some ups and downs, the true soldier survives, and simply stated, the soldier of Christ is victorious. So despite what people say or do, know that God can fight your battle!

"No weapon that is formed against thee shall prosper. . . ."

Isaiah 54:17

ins

I shall … eavens
asking for deli…

For my soul is taunted by
the deadly, by evil, and corruption of mankind.
I ask God why am I left
here in this battle of war.

For yet the Lord replies,
"To bear the pains for a future generation
and mistakes of your forefathers!"
But I still rejoice
even in the midst of my suffering.
God still comforts my soul,
feeds my body, and nourishes my soul.
O great is the living God!

For I stand among men and women of war
to battle for a country of a great land,
and yet I find only God has been
my rescuer throughout this battle of time.

Amen.

Save Me on the Battlefield

Bullets ring through the air
as I sit here on the battlefield.
When I return from this war, who will care.
Yet I fight continuously, and only God is my shield.

Two nations at war over power,
instead of what's right or wrong.
People lose their lives in the process
giving us no glory or a place in the world to belong.
This war is a midnight terror to survive on the
battlefield, I confess.

O God, save my soul,
just in case I'm wounded and die.
Mass destruction is what I see,
but I look forward to the streets of gold.
I'm barely hanging on, hoping not to cry.

I see the evil in people's hearts.
O save my soul, my gentle Savior!
I stand here avoiding hell's metal darts.
Just take me higher,
once I finish this mission of labor.

I Found a Friend on the Battlefield

I'm dressed in blue and white,
a brilliant soldier I am,
ready to go to war and fight
on behalf of my country who doesn't give a damn.

I'm tall, slim, and black,
tough looking and kind of ugly, too,
first round pick of the pack
to join the army crew.

Off to war I go,
naive of Jesus Christ.
Soon I discover who's my friend and foe.
No need to explain -
Jesus, He's my friend, my shield, and the one who
saved my life for a price.

Glory be to Him!
I'm back at home, all in tact.
If it were not for Jesus,
I would have died and that's a fact.

NAM

NAM, that's where I've been
fighting a war for my country
and killing lives. Was it a sin
to go to battle to clean up someone's dirty laundry?

NAM, that's where I've been
to defend a land
who has forgotten me
in a war that I had to withstand.

NAM, that's where I've been
standing proud for my country's glory
and going to war to win.
I am the victim with an untold story.

NAM, that's where I've been
honored with a purple medal
to pin
and left with my emotional state unsettled.

NAM, that's where I've been
to fight a dirty war
with other forgotten men.

NAM, that's where I've been.

WAR or WARFARE

I just got back from NAM,
no job in sight and no respect.
I was a prisoner for my country
and all I did was fight.
For I am a tall, black man
who stood on the firing line.
Yet I'm back at home and I see
innocent victims dying in the streets.
I'm confused and just don't understand.
I went to war for my country on the
principles of injustice
and yet injustice lies at home.
Oh why innocent blood was shed
for something so vain.
Now I've learned to put my trust in Jesus,
not in my country or the war.
The real war is not politics
but good and evil.
That's the real war -- Warfare, that's the war
from the enemy, the war of Satan - that's all,
the war of good and evil.

Grandma's Battlefield Prayer

Oh my Jesus, Oh my dear Jesus,
I'm living in terror and fright.
My windows have bars
and I'm enslaved as a criminal.
Oh my Jesus, Oh my dear Jesus,
can you please free me from this plight?

I lay down at night
while gun shots ring through the air.
I pray it doesn't hit my little grandbaby
or just some innocent victim.

Oh Jesus, Oh Jesus,
can you hear my prayer?
Please deliver me, I declare.
I need you, I need your powerful hand
to overcome this battle and withstand.

Oh wrap your arms around me
and my little one.
Pour down your anointing on us,
and the blood of Jesus.
Anoint us, Oh Lord!
Free us, Oh Lord!
Give me the strength to
stand on this battlefield
until our day comes to meet you.

Oh Jesus, Oh Jesus, Oh Jesus!
I know you're there, I know you're near me.
Your presence has been made known.
Your body has been my shield
while the bullet bounced off my home.
Thank you, Jesus, for another night
on the battlefield.

Go Tell Somebody

Go tell somebody
what Jesus has done for you.

Grandbaby
go tell somebody
that you're in the land of the living and
breathe for one more night.

Grandbaby
go tell somebody
how your forefathers and foremothers
plowed this land under a whip and fright.

Grandbaby
go tell somebody
what Jesus has done for you.

Tell them how Grandma washed white folks'
floors making them shine bright.

Grandbaby
go tell somebody
how Jesus passed the bill of Civil Rights.

Go tell somebody
how Grandma worked hard to send you
to college to work hard in that corporate
world.

Go tell somebody
that soon discrimination will come back--
reverse that is in a swirl.

But Grandbaby,
just tell somebody
about the God you serve will help you with
another battle you must fight.

Just tell somebody,
your children's children
and all their children,
so it won't be forgotten
of what Grandma told you.

Just tell somebody,
when I close my eyes
to see Jesus
just tell somebody,
yes, what we've been through.

Life in a Jar

I'm living in a war,
a war which no one can understand,
living behind a glass jar
in a mighty land.

The lid is fastened tight,
unable to breathe fully
my rage inside wants to fight
because the majority is the bully.

I must maintain my dignity and manhood
while my woman stands beside me,
pushing me, supporting me, telling me
I can and should.
For Jesus has died and set me free.

I will not surrender into defeat
because Jesus is my armor and sword,
and I cannot get beat
because He's paid the price for me to be
lifted aboard.

Many look through the glass
and know not what they see,
a man who was once locked in and harassed
but Jesus gave me the key.

No longer am I in a war
locked in a tiny jar.
For I'm free from hell's bars
and with Jesus in my life,
I know He's never far.

Only a Warning

You see, I've been spending time in prison for a crime I didn't commit. I often wonder why God put me here - to preach the gospel like Paul or to see the destitution of other men. Why Lord, just tell me why Lord, am I here? My eyes are opened to the lost, the bewildered, to the meanness, the contrition, and the evil of men. Tell me what must I do here. Just tell me why must I stay locked up in this cell for five years of my life for a crime which I didn't commit? Then before I knew it, a shining light appeared before me. It was the spirit of the Lord, warning me of what life would be like for the next 20 years if I didn't turn my life around. For it was only a warning, only a warning to show me that life could be bondage if I didn't follow Jesus' will.

I fell on my feet worshiping God, asking for forgiveness, and that shining light disappeared. Now you see I didn't do a crime against the law, but I had forsaken some of God's commandments: backbiting, fornication, even blasphemy, and this is why I was really here. I confessed my sins and within one hour, I was released from prison not because of the law of the land but because God forgave me and made a way for freedom.

So brothers, think about the times you didn't get the rap, God was trying to tell you something. And brothers, those of you who got convicted and were innocent, maybe there's something in your lives that you are guilty of in the eyes of God's laws.

Who Is Your God?

27 years I've been here
behind these prison walls.
Haven't seen freedom in a long time,
I wonder what it's like.
You see I'm a black man behind bars
locked away from society
because I was armed and dangerous.
Oh how could this be
when I knew I was safe in the Lord.

Has God forgotten me?
Oh how I call upon your name Allah!
Oh please hear from me,
I'm sitting here locked up behind these bars.

Then suddenly, I realized
that I had been praying to a false God.
So I started praying to God Almighty,
yes, the God who was incarnated in Jesus Christ.

Yet it is year 28
and I feel freedom again
outside of those bars.

God Has No Respect of Persons

Here I am sitting in prison
for a rape I committed.
I didn't do this crime
but yet I'm locked up behind bars
like an animal ready to go in a rage.
My dignity lost and I'm severed
from my family. Oh what can I do?
The system says guilty
but I know I'm innocent,
falsely accused - another Black man.
I am treated unfairly but thank God
Almighty that God is fair and
has no respect of persons.
God doesn't care if you're short, tall, ugly,
Black, White, or even Chinese--
only that you believe in God,
and that's just what I did.
Day and night from my cell, I called
on Jesus, Jesus day and night I prayed.
Can you just hear me?
Forgive me for hating the White man.
I cried," Just please deliver me!"
And on the ninth day of my call,
that old white guard who patrolled my cage said,
"Son, I believe in you. I'm also a
child of God and I've put my own money to bail you
out so you can go free.
Thank God Almighty that God is a God who has no
respect of persons."

America

♪ America, ♪ America, ♪ America
oh how great this land is.

Yeah right, how great this land is.
I'm a young brother, a young brother
just out of jail on the streets trying
to make it. I'm angry at the system,
the world system.
I feel like I'm the forgotten.
Oh I can make every excuse
in the world: no father,
a drug abused mother,
and so on...
No one to guide and teach me
and yet trouble finds me.

Well, I've made a change!
I was 19 and had been exposed
to every thing you could think of:
drugs, honeys, sex, booze,
jail, stealing and robbing folk.
And yet, the only thing that changed
or saved my life was God the Father.
It was a deacon from an old Baptist
church who led me to Christ. I realized that
I had the best Father in the world.

It was God Almighty,
the heavenly Creator,
who took me just like I was,
a filthy rag, who loved me,
protected me, and found me a home.

Now I'm 25, college educated
and working, and if it wasn't
for God, my main Man,
my Alpha and Omega,
I guess Satan
would have had another soul.
My brother, don't let Satan
give you an excuse.
Just remember Psalm 27:10,
"When my father and mother forsake me,
then the Lord will take me up."
And that's just what God did for me!

God Won't Forsake You

Yo, I'm the new homeboy on the block,
just moved into the neighborhood and
looking for a group to hang with.
Woe, the bloods look nice
or maybe the other crew.
What shall I choose?
What shall I do?
I'm just looking to fit in.
No parents to give me advice or direction.
Mom works all the time and
Dad nowhere to be found in years.
I need some love
and yet the gangs look like the right place.

So one night, I put on my sneakers
and went to the corner store
to get a snickers bar
        and five gang members
        got blasted,
        ages 10, 11, 12, and others 15.

Well, I'm only 13 and I sure do want
to grow up before I die.
So I went home and I prayed,
"God, Oh God just help me out."
And suddenly the next day,
an elder from that old wooden white church
approached me
saying, "Son I got the key.

I got the answer.
There's a youth program for you.
We'll help you.
We'll teach you about Jesus.
We'll educate you, and
there are other kids there your age.
Would you come and check it out?"

Then suddenly, I went to that
youth program and I found out
that this old wooden white
church had it going on.
I was able to rap, not to
street violence but about
the Lord and how God will help
you out if you turn to Him.

Thank God for that elder
who took a little interest in me.
And yes, also of course, God,
yes, the Almighty God, for
filling the shoes of my earthly father.

A Message to the Wounded Brother

The lost child,
        the forgotten child,
                the man of strength,
        the Black man at war,
the victim who suffered the many earthly bruises of this world!

Does not the Father hear your pain?
        Does not the Father feel your frustration?
Cannot the Father see your iniquity?

Turn from yourself,
my brother,
        lift your hand to Jesus,
and once again your power shall be restored.

The Black Man

Many of you are wondering what I feel in the inside:
torn down, ripped apart, and full of low esteem.
This is me a Black Man,
a man who suffered the injustice of this world.
But I fret not because I'm a child of God.
No longer do I put my worries in a system of
economics which has ostracized me.
No longer do I subject myself to the powers and
worries of this world.
No, not any longer,
but where I place my power is in the hands of the
Lord.
This is me a Black Man,
a child of the Nile
who crossed the mighty river
and found freedom,
not on a declaration sheet
but in the power of God above.

So what if you feel locked down!
So what if you feel down trodden and afflicted!
So what if you're a Black Man locked up in jail!
So what if you're a Black Man in America!
In God's eyes, God has no respect of persons.
And you know what?
God wants you,
and God is trying to get your attention.

So Black Man smile
and know that one day you will receive a crown,
an eternal crown because you have been
a warrior through the Red Sea
and even through the Nile.
But one day repent,
yes repent my brother,
and the vision of the Lord shall
appear to you in all His righteousness.
So repent, God knows your name,
and is calling you,
the Black Man.

Chapter 2

✦✦✦✦

Abuse in Society Is a Means Which the Devil Uses

Prologue

Abuse, it happens frequently in the home, this act of domestic violence. We can turn a page in any major city's newspaper and see reports of a domestic killing or battering. Abuse, this thing sent by the devil is used to break up families and cause torment. Abuse and domestic violence come from the pits of hell as devices to kill, steal, and destroy souls. In many households across America, women and children are victimized by live-in boyfriends, friends, or even husbands. Some who commit these acts of violence are motivated by the desire for power, control, drugs, or money. If you are driven to violence by any of these reasons, or if you are a victim, you should seek help. Many deny that they are in an abusive situation because they fear what others will say or think. By speaking out and getting help, you can save your life as well the lives of your children.

Many times God has made an out for God's people, and then Satan removes the seed of faith replacing it with fear. 2 Timothy 1:7 says, *"For God hath not given us the spirit of fear; but of power, and of love, and of a sound mind."* Has God made an out for you that you can't see because fear has such a hold on you that it clutters your mind with thoughts of inadequacy and helplessness? Do you say to your self, "I can't make it on my own?" Well, Psalms 37:25 NRSV says, *"I have been young, and now am old, yet I have not seen the righteous forsaken or their children begging bread."* What the Lord wants us to do is trust in Him. Statistics show that domestic violence is on the rise, and these acts of violence have killed many innocent victims, sometimes leaving children without parents. Domestic violence has led others to cry, mourn, and weep. God wants us to live long, prosperous lives, but we must trust in God and in God's plan.

Some people think that domestic violence is always perpetrated by a man to injure a woman, but there are many cases where women have injured men. In some situations, a woman has been known to have fallen under a fatal attraction spirit, stalking, harming, or even killing a man. In domestic violence, the victim can in fact be the woman as well as the man. God wants to take you out of these situations. Exodus 20:2 says, *"I am the Lord thy God, which have brought thee out of the land of Egypt, out of the house of bondage."* However, so many of us want to return to the Pharaohs in our lives, thinking that things will get better. Although I am in no way recommending or suggesting divorce of a spouse, but sometimes the abusive spouse needs time alone with God for reconciliation first so that he or she may rectify the inner-self.

Today ask yourself, “Am I in a domestic situation with a violent person?” Maybe the abuse is not physical; maybe it's verbal with the potential of leading to something violent. You must ask God for direction. Proverbs 3:6 states, *"In all thy ways acknowledge him, and he shall direct thy paths."* Trust in God and God shall open a door. God has called us to freedom and doesn't want us to be in bondage. Seek God’s will and the Holy Spirit will guide you. The following poems and short stories are based on real life situations; however, the names are fictitious. Do you see yourself in any of these situations? If so, God wants to deliver you, but remember, obedience is the first step toward deliverance.

Amen.

"I am the Lord thy God, which have brought thee out of the land of Egypt, out of the house of bondage." *Exodus 20:2*

An Angel in Distress

For my soul was taunted with rage
by an angry, violent man.
He slapped me, he beat me,
leaving marks of shame.
Oh how I yelled and yet I hoped
for my neighbors and loved ones
to beck for my call.
There I was, lying on the floor
beaten by a stranger
of a man I lived with
for more than eight years.
Oh God can you help me?
Oh God can you hear my moans?
Just please remove me
from this act of violence.
Oh how I call upon thee!
Just lift me up
so that I may see
life is more than a beating by my
mate, my love, and my husband.
Angels of fire
remove thy wicked hands.

So then, my body
lay there waiting, just
waiting for deliverance.
And soon an angel appeared before me
and reached out his hand,

"Come my child,
for there is yet deliverance
waiting for you.
For you are not alone.
Wipe thy eyes and
God will lead thy way.
For God on most High has heard thy plea.
You must know that God is by thy side,
and no one can touch thee
if thou will submit to Him.
For God has called you to peace.
Surrender and say thy word."

There I was in an unconscious
state, and I surrendered
to Jesus asking Him to be
the King of my life.
Instantly, the door bell rang
with paramedics, reviving me,
and their reply,
"Only seconds you were away from death!"
And then I saw the angel of peace pass by,
O dear Lord, my Savior,
I thank you on most High!

Satan Comes to Kill, Steal, and Destroy

1:00 AM sirens ring.
Oh my God, I wonder if something
terrible has happened.
People are running down the street.
Oh no, they're running toward my house.

Jesus, I yelled, oh Jesus let it not be my baby.
Yes it was, it was my three month old baby,
stabbed and cut up by my 15 year old son.
Jesus, I screamed, Jesus, I screamed.

Oh my Lord, why has evil knocked on my door!
Please deliver me out of this hell hole.
Then one thing I discovered,
it was Satan who possessed my son for
a minute. I know it was. I know it was!
Some of you just don't believe the enemy's power.

If I had only joined that church
on the street corner, maybe God would have
gotten to him first.

My Neighbor

It was early evening,
the kids were at school
and it was me all alone.
Suddenly, I heard a knock and then another.
It was an imposter, a robber.
Soon, I ran for my gun and shot him.
I took off his mask
and discovered it was
my neighbor.

My neighbor,
the one who I trusted with my kids,
the one who I spent many years talking to,
the one who I let inside of my house
and entertained at dinner,
the one who I gave my trust to,
the one who I've shot
and discovered he was the enemy all the while.
My neighbor, my neighbor!

Vengeance Is Mine

"Vengeance is mine," said the Lord.
But oh, I'm going to get mine.
Revenge I say is what it's all about.
I don't need no church or no God.
I am in control,
that's what I said.
I'm in control.

Then one day, my mother was taken out.
And only my Lord brought me about,
letting me know that God is in control.
You see God, yes God,
that's what it's all about!

Should I Get Involved?

2:00 AM,
I heard a yell and a scream
and then a punch and a bam.
I wasn't sure if this was a dream.

I tossed and turned
and to sleep I returned
to be awakened by voices I heard.

It was my neighbor yelling for help
as the husband beat her.
The blows so loud, her pain I felt,
couldn't believe she was a victim to this man
I thought to be a gentleman and sir.

Should I get involved?
Heavens no!
This crime, let the police solve.
Then I realized, as a Christian I must be a friend
not a foe but then, I was too slow.

Minutes later, I heard gunshots
Oh my God, I yelled.
Tell me what I've heard, it's not,
and then a body fell.

Oh, if I could have,
would have, or should have,
then my neighbor's life might still be!

Don't Let the Macho Man Send You to Hell

Rushing home from work,
bam the door slams.
This wife of mine
gets me so sick,
and now she wants to leave me.
How dare she do this thing
after all the time I spent in this marriage,
working hard to take care of her
and her illegitimate child?
And this is what she's going to do to me.
Oh, I'll take care of her.

No one messes with Big Moe.
As soon as she walks through
that door, I'm going to kill her.
Bam, the door swings,
bam the gun goes off,
and dead was my wife.
This was my story.

I can tell you the devil made me do it.
I can tell you it was I
who was afraid of losing her,
and not knowing how to deal with my anger.
Oh, I can tell you a lot of reasons.
For now she's dead, no mother
for my children, neither a father,
I'm in jail.

But one thought I have,
if I had gone to church
my life wouldn't be as miserable
because now she's with Christ,
and oh well,
I'm in hell with the devil;
all because of my proud manhood
thinking I was the head and
had to be in control all the time.
Now I'm in hell while she's living with Jesus.
So, I guess that sometimes being a macho man
can send you to hell.

She's a Special Gift

Joe Brown, the name, tall, good looking, young, and Black, smooth talking corporate arena man with the educational degrees of many, you name it: BA, BS, MBA, including PHD, successful with three kids and a wife fine as a golden Madonna. Two things I lacked were respect for women and knowledge of God. You see God blessed me with all the things I asked for, and yet the most sacred gift, a woman who is sweet as a honeycomb, the woman I abused, the woman I mistreated, the woman who I almost killed when I lost my job.

Well brother, it wasn't worth all of that to lose my soul and end up in hell. For I lost my job, my home, my car, and my family. Then I discovered that it was only Jesus who allowed me to get it all back. Well you know that sister, that beautiful auburn breeze, yes my special gift from God, my wife, the one I mistreated is back, getting from me the kindness, the love, and the treatment a queen deserves. For I'm thankful to God for bringing her back.

Look Up to Jesus

Man, I just don't understand how the world abuses you. You see my wife is pregnant for the third time and next I lose my job, and money is so tight, and at times I sort of lose it, beating her up. I just can't feed another mouth. I go to the unemployment line and still can't find a job. My life feels like its over and I have nowhere to turn. My wife nags and to shut her up, I slap her in the mouth, letting her know who's in control. She runs for that old black Bible, the one my mama gave to me saying, "Son, when life's not going the way you expect, just look up to Jesus." I didn't want to hear that. I'm a man who's trying to make it to feed this family of mine. Uncle Sam is on my back and Lord, the bills are so far behind. Then comes my wife who says, "Baby, just trust in Jesus." This time I slapped her so hard, she fell against the wall and later the baby died.

Now I sit in jail and a voice comes to me saying, "Just look up to Jesus." And that's what I did. Jesus made me realize that all I went through was what I needed to look up and depend on Him.

Satan Comes in Many Forms

Oh, I'm a young brother and I met this woman who was dynamite, mind-blowing, looks, intelligent, and had a way with seductive words. You know my spirit was willing to walk away but my flesh couldn't. Her words so sweet, her body so scrumptious. And there I was, sinning every night. I just had to have this woman, but then I found out she was Satan in disguise. She was like a fatal attraction, stalking me, terrorizing my home and family, and damaging my car. I couldn't believe this type of thing could really happen. She threatened my life and then the ultimate, I found myself locked in jail because she filed charges on me. Yes, can you believe, of abuse? She claimed that I hit her and knocked her unconscious. Well, I've never hit a woman, and man, she faked the bruises. How can women be so cruel, I thought, but then I realized that Satan comes in all forms.

Brothers, take it from someone who was a victim, everything that looks good, talks good and feels good, if the Holy Spirit of God is not in them, then know it's Satan coming to destroy your life. Be on guard. For the Bible tells us to be on guard, and it is better to love the wife of your youth than to fall in the bosom of a stranger.

Tanisha

Tanisha is my name
and slinging is my game.
You see I'm used by the devil
to kill, steal, and destroy
your living soul.
This is my game
and from the pits of hell I came.
Beauty I 'm filled with
and to bed I take you to get bit
because you are a fool
and I know you are weak
and don't always go to Bible school.
You see I'm the woman who you search for
fine, slim, pretty, and all that in a bar
waiting to capture and steal your soul
because you have forgotten your goal.
I'm ready to devour and eat you up
making you like me - all corrupt.
Can't you see I'm a trick of the devil?
Yet you come back to me.
Tell me why,
just why,
aren't you faithful like me
at God's name
as I am at Satan's game.

One Too Many

The door bell rings
at 2:00 in the morning,
oh who can this be,

Ms. Thing
or
the whore

who I took to bed and scored!

Bam she knocks louder on my door
and dead I was lying on the floor.

Eyes waking up in hell
because of a soul I stole and tried to sell.

Now everyday I scream and yell
in the burning fires of hell.

I got one too many honeys
without repenting to the Lord Almighty.
This is true, and hell, my brother, is nothing funny.

God Protects the Little Ones

I was a young girl
abused by all my mom's men friends.
This week Johnny,
next week Bryan,
next month Arthur,
never knew who was next.

Mother allowed this
just to have money in her pocket.
I didn't know who Jesus was,
I didn't go to church.
For this was forbidden in my household.
You see Jesus talked to me in my sleep
and said, *"I'll protect you no matter what."*
and soon I found myself free
living in a shelter for foster children.

Oh boy, do I know Jesus now!
I worship Him everyday because
He delivered me out of hell.

I've Been Delivered

a raped victim's story

For it was midnight on the hour,
the house in darkness and all was still.
Suddenly, I heard a knock at the door.
It was him again.
Oh no I yelled,
not another night
and he smiled, gazed into my eyes
and then a force of violence erupted.
Before I knew it, I was pinned against the wall
brutally raped time after time
until my body slid down the wall,
leaving me motionless as if I were dead.
The pain, the blood which ran down my legs,
the hurt, the pain of someone I loved so dearly,
the admiration I gave him, the hugs I gave,
the toys I received.
Oh, how could this be my father of 15 years?

But I rejoice!
My body was touched but not my soul.
God redeemed me,
fulfilling me with the power of the Holy Ghost.
Now I'm free of that midnight terror.
I'm free and may God get the glory.
I've been delivered!

A Brother's Pain Is Now Joy

I am the man who walks alone
afraid and frightened of the world,
not sure if I can succeed.
I cry at night when no one is around
hiding the pain inside
from being abused.
It's something not talked about much.
No, because I'm a man.
I'm tough, I got to take it,
and block out my angry feelings.

I am the man abused
who sat in a closet
keeping this secret quiet
from others.

I am the man abused
filled with shame.
To block out my pain
of this injustice,
I turned to a drug
thinking this would help me.

Oh I am the man who was abused
as a little 5 year old.
I am the Black man locked
into a certain sadness
but I'm delivered,
free from Satan's wicked hand.

You can't hold me in this
pain or certain sadness.
God, oh yes my heavenly Father,
has delivered me
freeing my body from the
torture and my offender.
I pray for you too
that you shall one day get freedom.

I'm no longer the victim.
I'm free in the spirit of God.
And though I hurt, I don't hate you.
I love you, brother, hoping you will
refrain from Satan's hand.
The weapon you formed against me
won't prosper.
I'm a child of God and I'm free.

Thank God Almighty!

Thoughts for the Moment

What makes a man become enraged
to beat his woman he loves
after making silly promises when they became
engaged?
Oh how to him, she's nothing more than a
punching glove?

Is it what he's taught
or simply angry with the world for what
he's not?
For a wife is a gem and not an item bought.

God Is Able

Pat is my name, once a welfare mother with three kids. All I wanted in life was to get that happy home and a man to take care of me to fulfill my every need. And that's just what I got, a beautiful Romeo, a beautiful Don Juan, tall, dark, handsome, driving a Benz with plenty of money.

My problems were over in life. He swept me off of my feet and even married me. I, thinking he was God-sent to have married a welfare mama like me with three kids. Oh, this tall, beautiful, bronze, candy-coated, sugar smackin' man, just to look at him would make me glitter! Oh, I idolized this man, making him King. He gave me fine clothes and glamorous meals, wining and dining. Kids had things they never had before.

I made it from the projects to the big house. I was no longer a welfare queen but Mrs. Society, driving luxurious cars. I had made it. I was no longer Patricia Brown and I was now Mrs. Patricia Ramirez. I was all that!

Then suddenly, after two years of this good living, my man Joe began mistreating me, calling me names which I can't repeat, that I was nothing and look at you, you're all fat. Why does a man like me need a fat woman like you. I couldn't believe this was my prince in shining armor speaking to me. Oh well, I thought.

The next day he came home early from work when the children were gone, slapping me, beating me, punching me, and even stabbing me in my side. Oh, you know, I took this for about three years, this abuse. Oh, why did I take it so long? Was it the good life and the riches I never had before? Was it for my children so they could have a father? Was it because I was fat, overweight and thought this was my last chance? What was it? It was me, not knowing that Jesus was Lord of my life. It was me, not knowing that God is my redeemer. It was me, not knowing of my sins committed and removing God out of my life.

Then, I discovered an old Baptist church, small in size with an old, grey-haired preacher and only about 20 members. Oh, that church set me on fire, making me realize that God is a true and living God. Oh, and for weeks, I would go to church and on my return home he, my husband, would beat me. The beatings came and I still went to church. I began to be filled with the Holy Ghost, and asked God to forgive me for my sins, renew my mind and body, be God of my life, remove the cup of abuse from my bitter lips, and I would worship God each and every day.

That night when I went home, my husband, the devil had that knife in his hand. And I said, "Satan, I rebuke you and be gone. For I am a child of God renewed in the spirit. I don't need you and none of your false ways. Jesus is Lord of my life. Be gone!"

And as he approached me coming toward my face, you know God stepped right on in, and that husband of mine before he could strike me, dropped dead of a heart attack. My sisters, I know that God is able!

Chapter 3

✦✦✦✦

Drugs in Our Society, What Are We Going to Do About It?

Prologue

*O*h why do so many in our community suffer from drug abuse? This is the question that many often ask. You see, drugs are another deceptive device used by Satan to steal, kill, and destroy God's people. For Satan comes in many forms, forms we ourselves take for granted. Many of our sons and daughters have been introduced to drugs in places least expected: the school grounds, the parks, in social groups, and organizations. We must confront this issue as an attack by Satan on God's people. It's not the government's role to take charge of our individual weaknesses, but ours. It is time for us to stop blaming others. It is we, ourselves, who are to blame. The Bible says to help those who are weak or feebleminded. It is our role as Christians to preach the gospel and be a light to the world. We must be living examples of Christ.

We must teach our children that drugs are, in fact, bad fruit, the fruit of death. Drugs impact our lives, our families, and our communities, therefore leaving future generations with curses of poverty, oppression, and everlasting pain. From their birth, we must preach to our children that their bodies are the temples of the Holy Ghost. Satan's job is to deceive our children, making them think what's good is bad, and what's bad is good. How are we going to prosper as a nation? Just because dugs aren't in your home doesn't mean that they won't affect your grandchild on the way to school when he's gunned down over $20.00. Just because drugs aren't in your neighborhood doesn't mean that you aren't the prey for slaughter at the gas station or the grocery store. You are the prey! What are you going to do as a Christian to save a soul, sit back or stand up? Drugs, these terrible chemicals produced to kill the end-user or the passerby! We are all victims. I suggest that you stand up and fight the enemy instead of letting it attack you.

". . . know ye not that your body is the temple of the Holy Ghost which is in you, which ye have of God, and ye are not your own? For ye are bought with a price: therefore glorify God in your body, and in your spirit, which are God's."

1 Corinthians 6:19-20

The First Step

I'm hooked on this drug
just can't seem to get off it.
Oh what is it?
I want to do better but
I just can't let it go.
I've been to rehab
yet I come back to it again,
oh why do I live on this pipe,
giving my body for sale.
Oh, I hate myself,
but this drug calls me back for more.
I want to make a change but I feel
so weak Lord.
Just tell me what I must do!

*"For you have made the first step and
that was to acknowledge me."*

It Takes One Step for God

This drug, I don't know why, I just
had to have it: in the morning,
at noontime, and in the evening.
I couldn't face the fact that I was
a functioning drug addict
going to work each and every day,
making money but giving it to Satan.

For God has blessed me with
a family, a beautiful wife, children,
a home, and a job. I guess I sort of
was throwing the blessings back in God's face.
Then I discovered this drug clinic which
gave me a twelve step program to recover.
But recovery for me was not only this twelve step
program, but the one step program
which is God the Father.
One taste of Jesus fulfilling my soul with
the Holy Ghost and God's power delivered me.
Try it for yourself because it worked for me and
it can work for you too.

God Bless!

A New Addiction

My life was a drug because I lacked something,
something, oh I don't know, maybe love and
a hug, or maybe something I tried to hide.
My self-esteem was lowered by others.
My self-esteem lessened because of my
inadequacies.
And through my drug, I discovered
a false sense of hope and truth.
For the drug controlled my mind
by, of course, Satan.
But I was able to overcome this addiction
by finding a new addiction
who was my Lord and Savior.

This new addiction, oh it has a
savoring taste in my mouth.
Oh this new addiction makes me jump
for joy in the morning and evening.
Oh this new addiction opens doors for
me that no one can close.
Oh this new addiction is awesome!

Do you want some of what I got?
Try it and you won't go back.
Oh my addiction is so powerful,
so overwhelming that it brings
glory and eternal life.
Oh this addiction that I have
is my sweet Lord and Savior!

I Was All of That

Oh there I was, tall, young, and black
thinking I was all of that
until suddenly I discovered death,
yes death, the death of someone
who cuddled me,
someone who would give her last for me,
moms, my mother,
the one I would give my all for.

But I was young, young, tall, and black
thinking I was all of that
running with the drug crew
thinking this was the best thing I knew
until I didn't fulfill my request
and soon I found my mother dead,
the one I loved best,
all because of a drug
and running with the thugs.
But now I know that God was getting my attention
so I could get saved
like my mother who was taken early to her grave.

Well, you know what,
God got my attention
and now I have been saved and received salvation.
Get on track my brothers and sisters!
It's nothing nice to lose your sweet old mother
behind a drug that doesn't offer love.
For only Jesus can do it from above!

Who Do You Choose?

Arnold is my name,
back from prison
on a drug use offense.
Sitting in prison,
I realized some things
that there's more to life
than the marijuana and cocaine I used.
It made me realize
that the enemy, yes Satan,
was trying to conquer my life.
Satan, the devil, was trying to destroy me
over a substance that would
control my mind, make me lose my job,
my wife and family.
This drug was taking me to hell.
But praise God, the Almighty God
who delivered me from this habit
in one night!
God asked me the question,
"Who do you choose, Me or Satan?"
And I chose God, and
free I was, not only
from the jail cell but
from the physical and mental
bondage which took hold of my life.
No more pain for me tied
to a drug and living in a cell,
but free in mind, soul,
spirit, and body, all in Jesus Christ.

Alternative Substance

There I was Ms. Professional and did all the things which mama told me: go to church, get a good education, and get a good job. I had it all! I was young, good looking, and a top notch attorney. I had the live car and all the perks. For I was at the top of my world until one day I walked into my boss' office and he said, "Ann, congratulations! You're getting promoted to the elite group of management. You've made it to the inner circle."

"Wow," I thought, this is incredible. After working two years at the firm, I'm being promoted to managerial level. This could only be a dream come true. I thought of how I could be known throughout my field and represent some of the best clients in the world. My mind had totally taken off.

So, my boss leaned back in his chair and asked, "Ann, do you accept?"And I said, "Mr. Phillips, no I resign!" He said, "What, are you crazy? This position is paying $50,000 more than you're making now. Do you know how many people would kill for this position and status?"

"Absolutely, I know many would kill for this position. For I am a child of God and the riches, fame, and status in this company, in this world cannot compare to the wealth and riches my Father has in heaven. You see Mr. Phillips, I've been doing my homework and I've discovered that this inner circle is filled with cocaine, an alternative substance.

But you see, Hebrews 11:1 states, ". . . *faith is the substance of things hoped for, the evidence of things not seen.*" I cannot be a part of a circle that destroys the mind. I will not and can not be hooked and ruled by the devil. Therefore, the fancy job, the fancy office, I don't need them. **Somebody's got to make a stand, how about you?"**

Crack Up or Wake Up

Dancing on my feet
to a tune of a jazzy beat,

I noticed some men who were dressed all fine
as I sipped on a glass of wine.

There I was, at a party, tall, young, slim, and black
and my first introduction to crack.

This was all it took
before I was hooked.

My life had gone downhill
always needing this drug to get fulfilled.

Once, I sold my baby for a dollar.
My addiction so bad,
I tuned out her screams and hollers.

For I was now a drug mama
and my life was a living trauma.

For I was hooked on crack
with no sense of reality or fact.

My whole world was a drug,
looking at persons to mug.

Now, I owed my drug dealer money
and unable to pay, killed was my baby,
my sweetest honey.

I was deadened to the power of the Holy Ghost
and Satan had taken control almost.

For the Lord giveth and taketh away.
Jesus, I yelled, oh please deliver me today!

Then I felt His angels' blessed hands
lifting me above the troubles I had to withstand.

Oh Jesus I cried,
please, but please just give me one more try.

I was standing there
with nothing more to bear,
and He rescued me, giving me a new life
overlooking the strife.

My baby who I gave birth
a precious ruby she was worth.

Now she's gone away.
For the consequences of sin
are sometimes hard to pay.

All because of a drug called crack,
I'll never get her back.

But one thing I've learned --
Jesus is all I need,
He's my deliverer, conqueror, and protector.

This is not fiction but fact,
and with Jesus in my life,
I don't ever, ever need to sway back.

From Bondage to Freedom to Bondage

It was a cold winter night,
streets were dark and filled with blackness.
The stench of the ghetto was profound.
Nearby on a street corner,
I saw two men exchanging
what looked to be dope,
dope, yes dope, that's what I said.

My people, my people, wake up!
Why, just tell me why
we want to self-destruct,
and poison our minds?
Isn't this a country of freedom,
yet why we still live in bondage of slavery.
Drugs, a form of medicine used
to induct our minds with a controlling agent,
drugs, a form of slavery.
I don't know about you, I got my freedom papers.
No drugs for me.
Oh how Aunt Kizzy, Unclc George, and
Papa Little all died for me to be free,
free from the shackles on my hands and feet,
and free from the bondage of a drug
used to destroy and control my mind.
That's right, no drugs for me,
I'm free.

Addicted, Convicted, Restricted, With Your Mind Afflicted

You know my name,
and that's who I am.

Let me tell you my story
but I don't need your fame or glory.

I had a friend who used a drug
looking for love and a hug.

This drug offered him a lot of pain
and a mistake that can't be regained.

You see, he became addicted,
convicted,
restricted,
with his mind afflicted,

Making him do
what he wouldn't normally do.

He took his life
along with his lovely wife
because he was confused
and didn't know Jesus Christ.

Now he's dead
with another life taken in bloodshed
leaving others to cry, mourn and weep
because he thought this drug would make
him complete.

You see his wife, she was my girl, my cousin,
my friend who I loved,
now she's taken above.

Sometimes I cry over her grave,
but thanks to her, my life is changed
and now saved.

Now I've learned what a drug can do;
that's why I leave this message with you.

It can make you addicted,
convicted,
restricted,
with your mind afflicted,

Making you do
what you wouldn't normally do.

You see, this is my story,
not to make you worry;

But to make you understand what a drug can do,
and if you indulge, this may happen to you.

We Are the Prey

Oh how I sat on the church pew
overlooking your casket in my view.

First tears, then uncontrollable pain
of someone I lost, feeling empty with
nothing to gain.

Oh how the songs brought sorrow to my face,
Walk Around Heaven and *Amazing Grace*.

This pain so unbearable made me scream
of a nightmare that's now a reality which
I never dreamed.

The minister gave his final speech,
a comforting word that I could hold and reach.

The pallbearers carried you out
to the graveyard en route.

Riding in the limousine following your hearse,
my heart palpitated as if it wanted to burst.

I stood over your grave site
as the minister issued the final burial rite.

I placed one last flower
on your coffin to show my love in the last hour,

thinking about the pain you suffered
at the hands of a thug
whose problem was in a drug.

On this day,
I knew you were gone forever, yes passed away.
But when I looked to God, I knew you were
in heaven to stay.

For we are the prey,
yes, the prey,
and my brothers and sisters,
it's time to pray.

Chapter 4

✦✦✦✦

Don't Give Up, for the Battle Is Not Won!

Prologue

"Behold, I sit on my throne waiting to capture my wife. Are you ready?" said the Lord in my inner spirit. "In heaven, there is no more sorrow or pain. For I will come and wipe all tears away."

All works which you do for the Lord will be openly rewarded. God allows people to suffer need many times so that we know it's God who helps us. For if we have faith as small as a mustard seed, we can do many things. We have allowed Satan to cause fear and self-doubt. At times, we worry how bills are going to get paid or about an illness which has afflicted the body. But do you know that the scripture says, *"Let not your heart be troubled: ye believe in God, believe also in me."* (John 14:1), *"But my God shall supply all your need according to his riches in glory by Christ Jesus."* (Philippians 4:19), and finally, *"But he was wounded for our transgressions, he was bruised for our iniquities: the chastisement of our peace was upon him; and with his stripes we are healed."* (Isaiah 53:5).

God takes no pleasure in the person who draws back from Him. Hebrews 10:38 states it this way, *"Now the just shall live by faith: but if any man draw back, my soul shall have no pleasure in him."* We, as Christians, must be ready to face the challenges when they come knowing that we are the children of God and God shall supply our need, never leaving us comfortless. God wants us to have patience, knowledge, wisdom, hope, and faith in God. Doesn't God know what you're going to do before you do it? Doesn't God know what's going to happen before you do? God is all-knowing and omnipotent. You must know that all things work together as stated in Romans 8:28 NRSV, *"We know that all things work together for good for those who love God, who are called according to his purpose."* Don't give up on this race, the battle is not yours. Keep believing and know that God has a plan. Keep your eyes on Jesus and don't look back. Believe in God's word and God shall deliver. For God has heard your prayers. Don't give up; for the blessing is coming if you follow God's plan. Be strong and encouraged. Joshua 1:9 NRSV states, *"I hereby command you: Be strong and courageous; do not be frightened or dismayed, for the Lord your God is with you wherever you go."* So my brothers and sisters, continue to believe, trust, and have faith in God. Just, don't give up!

"Nay, in all these things we are more than conquerors through him that loved us."

Romans 8:37

"And let us not be weary in well doing: for in due season we shall reap, if we faint not."

Galatians 6:9

Put Your Trust in the Lord

I trusted in the Lord
and completion was in me.

I trusted in the Lord
and I found true happiness.
I trusted in the Lord
and leaned not unto my understanding,
and before me,
He granted a true reward.
I've learned to trust in the Lord
and therefore, I never go wrong
because He is almighty and glorious.

How about you,
who do you put your trust in?
Hope it's not mankind.
For people are not perfect,
                    not all knowing,
                    not all glorious.
But one who puts trust in the Lord
shall never go astray or wrong.

Amen.

I Trusted in Him

I trusted in the Lord
and He showed me a new way.
I trusted in the Lord
and He opened a new door.
I trusted in Him, oh yes I trusted in Him,
O how great and magnificent He is!

He led me not astray,
often I wondered and wasn't sure
but He always sent a sign
and showed that I was on the right path.
I trusted in Him with all my decisions
and discovered He was always right.

I trusted in Him, I trusted in Him,
and didn't I find the road to true prosperity.
You too should trust in Him
if wealth and happiness are what you desire.

Who Is He?

My god, my shepherd, my King, my Jehovah,
my love, my Emmanuel, my greatness, my truth, my
bright and morning star, my wisdom and
knowledge. Who is this person?

My God!

HE IS!

O how faithful HE IS!
O how trusting HE IS!
O how lovely HE IS!
O how peaceful HE IS!
O how godly HE IS!
O how holy HE IS!
O how good HE IS!
In the morning
        and in the evening,
He is holy and everlasting.

HE IS, LORD!

Thank You, Lord

I wake up in the morning to see the sun shine
another day.
Thank You, Lord!

I can see the birds fly in the air.
O Thank You, Lord!

I can walk today and hear the kettle blow.
Just Thank You, Lord!

I woke up in a sound mind ready to face the enemy.
Thank You, Lord!

Just Thank You Lord!
I Thank You Lord!
I Just Thank You
that your life and spirit was poured on me
another day.

I Got My Eyes on Jesus

I got my eyes on Jesus,
no matter what goes on.
I got my eyes on Jesus;
it doesn't matter what people say or do.
I got my eyes on Jesus,
don't care if the robbers break in.
I got my eyes on Jesus;
I don't care if I lose my job.
I got my eyes on Jesus,
and if I do just that
then nobody, no one, or no thing
can bother me
because I got my eyes on Jesus.

Only My Lord

Food on the table,
who did this?
Oh, its my Lord!

Gas in my tank,
who put it there?
Must be my Lord!

Clothes in my closet,
how it got there?
Had to be my Lord!

Money in my pocket,
Only my Lord,
my Lord, my Lord!

Knock on the Door

Knock on the door,
        who can it be?

Knock on the door,
        but I don't see anyone in my view.

Knock on the door,
        what can this be,
a bag of money when most in need.

Knock on the door
        footsteps gone away,
can't be nobody but the Spirit of my Lord.

God Is All You Need

I noticed cash was low.
        Oh no,
        what will I do?
A dollar in my pocket
        and hungry as I can be,
        what am I gonna do?
Tell me Lord,
        what am I gonna do?

God replied, "*Aren't I all you need!*"

Then suddenly, food came my way
        and hunger left.
Then money came my way
        and pockets were filled with cash.
Oh thank you Lord for being this way!

Jesus, the Change in My Life

For I have been led by the great shepherd of time. For He is the great one, oh yes the greatest of all mankind, of every creature. He is my Lord and Savior. You see many people wonder about the change which has come about in my life. I say unto you all, simply Jesus, oh yes, simply Jesus. You see when I wake, it's Jesus, and when I sleep, it's Jesus, just Jesus, the King of my life.

He's my Watchtower,
my Shining Star,
my King of kings,
and yes, my Lord of lords.

So you see the change in my life is just simply Jesus. That's all Jesus - just one word, I say unto you "Jesus," the main source, the main ingredient.

Glory be to Jesus!

What's My Purpose?

Oh I sit here on my window's ledge
wondering why God has brought me here.
What's my purpose,
I often wonder
what's my purpose?
Then I hear a voice which responds,
"to save others and witness
who God is."
And then I ask but to whom my Lord?
And again the voice responds:
"The little boy who plays in front of your door,
the garbage man,
the mailman,
the roofer,
the janitor,
all people who you confront.
This is your purpose,
just to tell the world about me.
It's simple - can't you see!"

What Is Truth?

My Savior who died on the cross
for the sins we bore.
O how great He is
from the hills to the mountains and valleys!
This is my God.
He lifted me to see
the greatness in Him
while I squandered in wrong places.
He showed me a clear path,
a clear path of truth.

Do you know a person without knowledge
is simply a fool,
simply a fool?

Greater is He that lives in me.
A person without knowledge
is a fool with no truth.
Knowledge is God and
God is knowledge.
Truth is He and
He is truth.
Therefore, God is truth.

O How Great Thou Art, Our Living God!

O how great thou art, our living God!
For He is ever wonderful.
He restored my feet from iniquity.
He comforted me when I cried.
He carried me when I was weak.
He lifted my soul when my spirit failed.
O how great thou art, our living God!
He shall be worshipped each
and every day.
He directs our steps
protecting us from evil.
He makes a table of food
to feed me when I hunger.
He remembers me even
in the midst of my sins.
Hosanna in the highest,
O how great thou art, our living God!
I shall worship Him each and every day
because thou on most High hast paved
the way!

Amen.

Chapter 5

✦✦✦✦

Eternal Life or Death, Which Do You Choose?

Prologue

*M*any people have seen the path of the wicked as well as the path of the righteous. It is a straight and narrow path to eternal life, but the path to destruction is wide and broad. Which path will you take? The book of Matthew speaks of this in chapter 7:13-14, *"Enter ye in at the strait gate: for wide is the gate, and broad is the way, that leadeth to destruction, and many there be which go in thereat: Because strait is the gate, and narrow is the way, which leadeth unto life, and few there be that find it."* For God comes to save that which is lost. Your time comes quickly. Are you prepared for your eternal resting place? Have you chosen to walk straight and narrow so that your name will be written in the Lamb's book of life?

Satan's job is to deceive you in any way to conquer your soul. The enemy's devices are very cunning. Satan may use an attractive woman or man to lure you; Satan may use a crack pipe to devour your mind so that he might compel you to do greater acts of evil; Satan may use competitive jealousy, strife, and/or confusion between you and your brothers and sisters to prevent you from receiving greater blessings by working as a team or in unison; Satan may use a false prophet - a person perpetrating to do the works of God, but who in reality is a ravening wolf seeking to do evil and destroy; or Satan may even use the media of television and music to send false messages subliminally to your mind. Revelation 20:10 says, "*And the devil that deceived them was cast into the lake of fire and brimstone, where the beast and the false prophet are, and shall be tormented day and night for ever and ever.*" Revelation 20:15 states, "*And whosoever was not found written in the book of life was cast into the lake of fire.*"

It's your choice to do right or wrong. For Jesus has come to pay for our sins. He died on the cross so that we may have a right to eternal life. Are you prepared? If today was your last day on earth, do you know where your eyes would open: heaven or hell, eternal life or death? The decision is yours; hope it's eternal life. Are you ready because the bridegroom comes quickly!

"And, behold, I come quickly; and my reward is with me, to give every man according as his work shall be. I am Alpha and Omega, the beginning and the end, the first and the last. Blessed are they that do his commandments, that they may have a right to the tree of life, and may enter in through the gates into the city."

Revelation 22:12-14

DEATH or LIFE

DEATH, that's the physical state of being no more.

DEATH, it may be called destruction or hell's door.

DEATH, a place filled with pain and agony.

DEATH, this is not where my Father is,

but LIFE is where God is eternally!

Are you prepared for DEATH or LIFE?

HATE

HATE, this thing sent by the devil
to destroy our people of color.

HATE, this thing sent by the devil
to cause confusion of the races.

HATE, this thing sent by the devil
to set a person's mind in confusion to
murder oneself.

HATE, this thing sent by the devil
to destroy a nation of God's people.

Thank God, God is LOVE
and overcomes HATE
with His power and glory.

HATE, this thing sent by the devil
to destroy opposing nations.

HATE, this thing sent by the devil
which lead men to disrespect women
and break up families.

HATE, this thing sent by the devil
to destroy God's people
can only be accomplished if you let
HATE rule in your life.

War and Violence

WAR and VIOLENCE,
that's what I said.
WAR and VIOLENCE,
everywhere I go
I see
WAR and VIOLENCE.

Everywhere I go
I see
WAR and VIOLENCE.
Thank God,
in heaven it's
LOVE and PEACE.

VIOLENCE

Violence, yes violence,
V-I-O-L-E-N-C-E.

Violence, my people infiltrated by this act of evil.
Has not the land God gave to you been resourceful
enough?
Oh how does a person take another life
over a drug!
Oh how one may steal from another
to gain for oneself the wants and
pleasures of this life!
Violence, that's what I said,
is the destruction of our people.
We, the inhabitants of this land
have allowed greed and disharmony to take over
our minds.

What's wrong my brothers and sisters?
A baby shot,
A baby murdered,
A baby raped!

Violence, just plain old violence.
Violence with a capital "V"
indicating vicious and vindictive.
Violence, where will it all end?
Hell, H-E-L-L, in the fires of hell
because that's where it all started!

Words Unto the Wise

The struggles of men and women are such few.
The wrath of mankind is yet so harsh.
Why doesn't a person see the understanding
of wisdom and the light which shines upon oneself?

Doest not the Father correct a child
when he or she hath sinned?
Lest I be fooled by your
discontented heart!
Verily, I say unto all mankind,
put away your shameful acts.
Then will peace flow into your hearts,
and long suffering may vanish from you.
For the world is a good thing
but what thou hast done
has made it yet an evil thing.
Unto the wise, pray always,
and unto the evil that lurks
onto city streets, behold,
your day to come is such a finite hour.
These words shall be clung to thy necks
as a cluster of chain.
Go in peace, my children.

Amen.

It Is Wise to Be Wise

Men and women are confused by the
acts which they perform.
Why should a person join a crowd
and know not what things are asked of one?
Why does a person not use discretion?

Have not I, the Father, given you
the power to reason?
Why does one feel alone when
one serves me - am not I there?
Behold, unto all of you who know
me not, for the time will come
when you will cling to your
loved ones and all things you desire
of this earth, and they shall disappear
from thy sight.
Behold, I say unto you, it is wise
to be wise and serve me.
For when destruction of war and doom
come unto you, I, the Father,
will hear not.

Hope It's Eternal Life

Do you know that ETERNAL LIFE is forever?
ETERNAL LIFE is where the Father is,
high above in the heavens
waiting to give you eternal glory.

What do you choose:
Peacefulness or Eternal suffering,
Glorified abundance or Torment of hell fires,
Serenity everlasting or Pain and suffering
continually,
Longevity or Death,
God or Satan?

Hope it's ETERNAL LIFE
because hell is where you will encounter strife.
Hope it's ETERNAL LIFE
because that's where God is.
Hope it's ETERNAL LIFE
because one day the bridegroom
is coming for His wife.
Hope it's ETERNAL LIFE!

My Soul Burns in the Fires of Hell

I've done something over and over again;
yet, I've failed and sinned.

Why does my soul submit to temptation
by what the evil one gives that's filled with
corruption?

Why am I so weak
and overtake the meek?

Why do I ponder on the elderly and kids?
Am I a lunatic of some sort
or out of my mind and wits?

For I'm the murderer, I'm the thief who robs
preying on souls.
I've submitted to the devil to gain hold of
treasures and gold.

I've stalked many yet my soul doesn't rest.
But now it's time to confess

that here in the fires of hell I suffer.
My soul consumed with grief and agony to discover

that it is better for a person to submit to the
Lord King,
and live eternally in heaven peacefully
where the angels sing.

For hell's fires
is no desire.

I pay the price
for doing wrong and
not following Jesus Christ.

In Death I Shall Live

I am the man who robbed, stole, and killed
just for a nickel or dime.
I am the man who robbed, stole, and killed
because I lacked knowledge of the Savior.
So here I sit in prison paying for my sins of wrong.
I sit locked behind bars in a cage like a raging
animal.

Now I await a death sentence because of
my hurt to society.
I was the man who robbed, stole, and killed,
but now I am the man who found the truth
of knowledge I lacked.
This knowledge, I say, this knowledge
was simply Jesus, my Lord and Savior,
because He has pardoned me.
I'm free in the inside
and this is all that matters.

Thanks be to God
that even God loves me,
the man locked in a cage,
but now tamed as a spiritual person.
Glory be to the Father,
in death, I shall live.

Old Drunken Red

2:00 A.M. bullets of a gun shoot my way.
I wonder if someone's dead.
Oh let me pray
that it wasn't old drunken Red.

One, two, three more shots in the air,
let me call 911.
Oh, I don't care.
I'm inside and so is my son.

Four, five, six, seven,
then eight, nine, ten more shots,
I feel like I'm living in a war.
Oh that's a lot.
Bullets nearby and not too far.

I gazed out of the window
and saw old drunken Red
sitting low
filled with blood, dead.

This man who I stepped over for years
never did any harm to me.
Am I like the rich man who passed over Lazarus?
Now it's all clear,
eleven, twelve, thirteen shots aimed at me.

Oh Lord, my eyes open in hell
while old drunken Red carried to heaven
while my body burns and yells,
all because I passed over old drunken Red
by years of seven.

I'll Be Prepared

I sit here reading my Bible at night
under my kitchen table light.

Some think that my life is boring and passing me by,
but I'm building treasures in the sky.

Why should I hope for a jackpot or magic seven
when my soul can be guaranteed in heaven?

Why should I sit at a casino table,
look at corruption on cable,
or bet on horses in a stable?
For God is truth and always able!

To some, I'm peculiar and rare,
but when my time comes, I'll be prepared.

I've learned not to put my faith in houses and riches
which can rust,
but in faith, honesty, and hope in God whom I trust.

So you see, I sit here reading my Bible at night,
always trying to do what's right.
And when my time comes as a thief in the night,
at the end of the tunnel my eyes will open to see
God's living light.

Heaven, That's Where I'm Going

Heaven, Oh heaven, that's where my Father is!
Heaven, Oh heaven, that's where I'm going if
I follow the righteous path!

You see heaven is where my real Father is.
The great Father who waters the land
and provides soil for food to grow.

You see heaven is where my Father lives
looking down on me as I walk this land.

Sometimes I stumble, and oh sometimes I fall,
but God's merciful hand picks me up,
shakes off the dust, and makes me walk tall.

You see, from heaven is where the sun shines bright
making me realize that God is the given light.

You see when I look to heaven, I can see God's
heavenly smile;
the smile that gleams on you and me.

I'm so glad that the Father lives in heaven
waiting on me to come home and be with Him.

You see heaven, Oh yes heaven, that's where I'm
going when my journey is complete!

Fly Away on Heaven's Wing

O heavenly host,
O how I call upon thee!
For thou hast taken me to greatest heights.
For it is only you whom I shall
worship unto the end.
O gracious God, my greatest God!
For thou wast my fortress
in time of war.
For thou fought my battle,
saving me from the enemy.
O how deeply I cried unto you,
and Father, thou answered
my prayers on cold winter nights.
I sat many nights in front of the firewood
waiting for the cold winter storm to
blow over.
O how I surrendered to you
and thou took me under your wing!
For I was glad when
thou took me on heaven's wing.

Bet on Christ

My God, the creator of the earth,
my God, the maker of the land!
O how all persons refuse to take a stand
for what is righteous.
Woe unto the one who has heard and finds me not.
For the earth will perish
but my words will stay.
Take my hand and join the Christian crew
so you won't be left feeling blue.
Know hell is of fire and hot with an
eternal flame,
but life everlasting is with God's fame.
Take my hand and follow the golden path.
Eternity with me is no mistake.
Bet on Christ for His name's sake
and I will allow thee to be in eternity,
yes, with the Father, the Son, and the Holy Ghost -
the Holy Trinity.